DATE DUE

SEP 0 2 2003	
JUL 0 8 2004	
AUG 2 6 2004	
FEB 0 6 2005	
JAN 2 3 2006	
AUG 1 5 2006	

DEMCO, INC. 38-2931

D1370205

The Piazza

Every Italian town has at least one piazza, or square. Italians love to meet and talk in the piazza.

A. Michelangelo and Galileo are buried in the 13th century church of Santa Croce in Florence.

B. The statue of a pope looks down on the citizens of Perugia as they catch the last warm rays of the setting sun on the steps of their cathedral.

C. Friends meet for a coffee.

D. Retired citizens meet each day in the piazza to discuss the latest news.

E. Meeting friends under a statue of Giuseppe Garibaldi, who joined the separate states of Italy into one country in the nineteenth century.

F. Soccer in the square.

Ancient Rome

A. Romans meet and talk in cafes in front of the Pantheon temple, which the Romans built in 27 B.C.

B. The Arch of the Emperor Constantine, who made Christianity the official religion of Rome, was built close to the Colosseum. Constantine made Christianity the official religion of Rome

C. The remains of The Roman Forum. The Forum was the center of government of the Roman Empire.

ITALY
the culture

Greg Nickles

A Bobbie Kalman Book

The Lands, Peoples, and Cultures Series

 Crabtree Publishing Company

www.crabtreebooks.com

The Lands, Peoples, and Cultures Series

Created by Bobbie Kalman

Coordinating editor
Ellen Rodger

Production Coordinator
Rosie Gowsell

Project development, photo research, and design
First Folio Resource Group, Inc.
Erinn Banting
Pauline Beggs
Tom Dart
Bruce Krever
Debbie Smith

Editing
Maggie MacDonald

Separations and film
Embassy Graphics

Printer
Worzalla Publishing Company

Consultants
Patricia Bucciero, Embassy of Italy–Ottawa; Carlo Settembrini, Italian Cultural Institute

Photographs
Mary Altier: p. 12 (both); Robert Arakaki/ International Stock: p. 9; Art Resource: p. 18 (bottom left); Fabrizio Bensch/Impact: p. 11 (bottom); Gerald Brimacombe/International Stock: p. 11 (top); Mark Cator/Impact: p. 5 (top), p. 13; Corbis/Archivo Iconografico, S.A.: p. 25 (top); Corbis/Bettman: p. 25 (bottom); Corbis/Araldo de Luca: p. 20 (left); Corbis/ Mitchell Gerber: p. 27 (top right); Corbis/Hulton-Deutsch: p. 27 (bottom); Corbis/David Lees: p. 7 (top), p. 24 (both); Corbis/Dennis Marsico: p. 15 (top); Corbis/Vittoriano Rastelli: p. 22 (right); Corbis/ Nicolas Saphieha/Kea Publishing Services Ltd.: p. 6 (right); Corbis/Claude Schwartz: p. 27 (top left); Corbis/Ted Spiegel: p. 14 (right); Corbis/Hubert Stadler: p. 5 (bottom left); Corbis/Mark L. Stephenson: p. 21 (top); Corbis/ Vince Streano: p. 29 (left); Corbis/Sandro Vannini: p. 15 (bottom); Peter Crabtree: front endpapers, back endpapers, title page, p. 4 (both); p. 7 (bottom), p. 8 (both), p. 10 (both), p. 16 (both), p. 17 (top), p. 21 (bottom), p. 28; Mario De Biasi/ Digital Stock: p. 23 (right); Georg Gerster/Photo Researchers: p. 22 (left); Wolfgang Kaehler: p. 3; Erich Lessing/ Art Resource: p. 17 (bottom); Richard T. Nowitz: cover; Willi Peter/Photo Researchers: p. 18 (bottom right); Reuters/Paolo Cocco/Archive Photos: p. 19 (top); Reuters/Luciano Mellace/Archive Photos: p. 6 (left); Reuters/Stefano Rellandini/Archive Photos: p. 18 (top); Scala/Art Resource: p. 19 (bottom), p. 20 (right), p. 26, p. 29 (right); Stevan Stefanovic/Photo Researchers: p. 23 (left); G. Veggi/ Photo Researchers: p. 14 (left)

Illustrations
Dianne Eastman: icon
Alexei Mezentsev: pp. 30–31
David Wysotski, Allure Illustrations: back cover

Cover: The Santa Maria della Salute church stands on the Grand Canal in Venice.

Title page: *The Nile*, sculpted by the Romans in the first century, is housed in one of the many galleries in the Vatican Museums.

Icon: Columns, which stand in many ancient Roman ruins, appear at the top of each section.

Back cover: The golden eagle lives in the Alps, a mountain range in the north of Italy.

Published by
Crabtree Publishing Company

PMB 16A,
350 Fifth Avenue
Suite 3308
New York
N.Y. 10118

612 Welland Avenue
St. Catharines
Ontario, Canada
L2M 5V6

73 Lime Walk
Headington
Oxford OX3 7AD
United Kingdom

Cataloging-in-Publication Data
Nickles, Greg, 1969–
Italy, the culture / Greg Nickles
p. cm -- (The lands, peoples, and cultures series)
Includes index.
ISBN 0-7787-9371-0 (RLB) -- ISBN 0-7787-9739-2 (pbk.)
1. Italy--Civilization--Juvenile literature
[1. Italy--Civilization.] I. Title. II. Series.
DG441.N57 2001
945--dc21
00-057075
LC

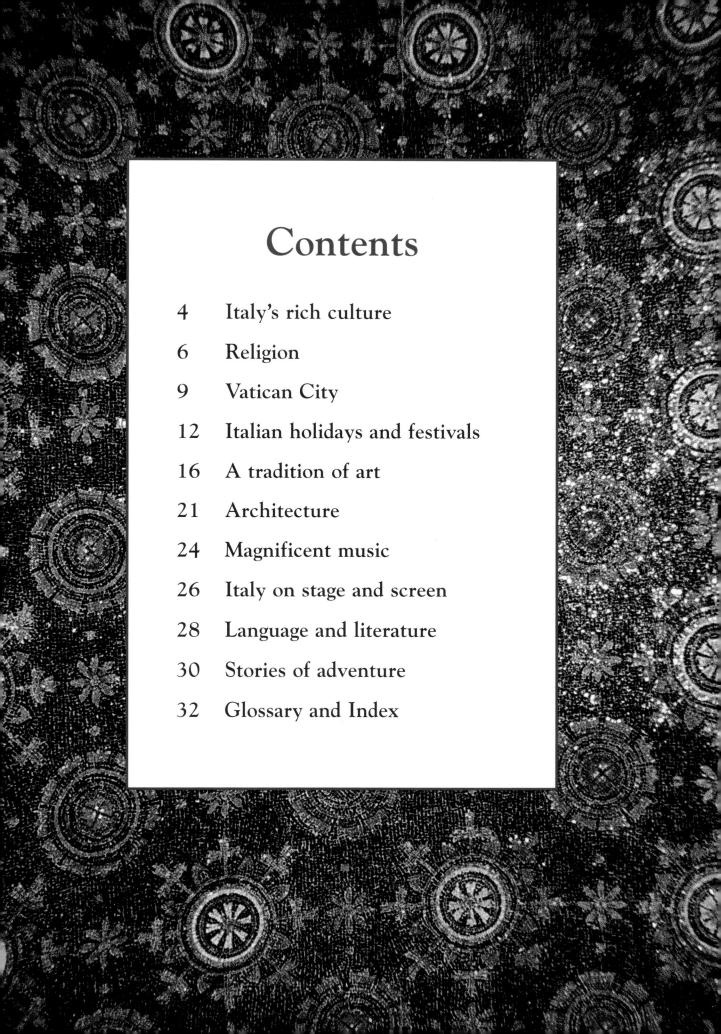

Contents

⛪ Italy's rich culture ⛪

Italy has one of the richest cultures in the world. The history, arts, customs, and beliefs of its people stretch back to ancient times. Since before the Roman Empire, which ruled Italy 2,000 years ago, powerful leaders have encouraged painters, sculptors, musicians, poets, and other artists to create masterpieces. For about 1,600 years, Italy has also been home to one of the world's major religions, Roman Catholicism.

Today, Italians share a great love for their arts, religion, and history. Italian cities are filled with old buildings and museums devoted to stunning artwork. Ancient Roman ruins stand throughout the land, as well as churches, **shrines**, and statues of heroes from history. Everywhere, people celebrate holidays and festivals to mark special occasions.

The exterior of Venice's duomo, or cathedral, is decorated with statues of saints. The cathedral was built in the 11th century.

Paintings that show historical and biblical scenes decorate many of Italy's buildings and churches. This painting shows Silvio Piccolomini of Siena meeting his future wife, Eleonora of Portugal, around the year 1450.

(above) During the **Regatta Storica,** *a parade in Venice, gondoliers and musicians dress in colorful costumes and ride in fancy gondolas.*

(above) People in costume perform a traditional folk dance at the **Feste del Tordo,** *a local festival in Montalcino.*

(right) The Arch of Septimus Severus was built in 203 A.D. Its ruins stand in the Forum, a public square in ancient Rome filled with temples, buildings, and monuments.

Almost all Italians belong to the Roman Catholic Church. Roman Catholicism is a **denomination** of Christianity. Only about two percent of Italians are not Roman Catholics. They include about a half-million Protestants, who follow other Christian beliefs. There are tens of thousands of Jews who live according to the teachings of a holy book called the *Torah*. Islam, a religion based on the teachings of the **prophet** Muhammad, also has thousands of followers.

What is Christianity?

Christianity is one of the world's major religions. It was founded about 2,000 years ago by followers of Jesus Christ. Christians believe that Christ was the son of God on earth. They also believe he was able to perform miracles such as healing illnesses and returning to life after he was **crucified**. Christ's life story and teachings are written in the holy book called the New Testament. Christians also consider another book, the Old Testament, to be holy.

*A synagogue, or place of Jewish worship and study, is decorated with marble carvings and special gold candlestick holders called **menorahs**.*

Roman Catholicism

Since its beginning, Christianity has branched into many denominations. Roman Catholicism was based in ancient Rome. It was one of the earliest denominations. Today, it has about a billion followers around the world. In addition to honoring Christ, Roman Catholics honor his mother, Mary. They also believe in hundreds of **saints**, people through whom God is said to have performed miracles. Local churches are led by priests, who devote their lives to the study and **worship** of Christ.

Leader of the Church

The priest who leads the Roman Catholic Church is called the pope. He lives in Vatican City, in the heart of Rome. The pope instructs Roman Catholics around the world how to live according to Christ's teachings. A pope holds his office for life. He is selected by a conclave, a special meeting of cardinals, who are high-ranking priests.

Karol Josef Wojtyla, known as Pope John Paul II, was chosen to lead the Roman Catholic Church on October 16, 1978. He was the first pope from Poland and the first non-Italian pope in 456 years.

Choosing the pope

Selecting a new pope can be a difficult task. Within eighteen days after the former pope's death, cardinals hold a conclave in a small section of Vatican City. They must stay in this area, which includes small apartments and a church called the Sistine Chapel, until they decide on a new pope. They are not allowed to speak with anyone outside the conclave and people outside the conclave are not allowed to speak with them.

Burning ballots

Cardinals usually select the new pope by election. Candidates are usually part of the conclave. Twice each day during the conclave, the cardinals meet in the Sistine Chapel to vote. After the ballots are counted, they are burned in a small stove. People outside watch for the smoke. To signal that they have elected a new pope, the cardinals mix dry straw with their ballots. This produces white smoke. If no one wins the vote, the ballots are burned with wet straw. This makes black smoke. Shortly after a successful vote, everyone emerges from the conclave and the new pope blesses the onlookers who have been waiting outside.

(above) The black smoke rising behind this statue in Vatican City indicates that the conclave has still not chosen a new pope.

(left) The Basilica di San Francesco in Assisi was built in honor of Saint Francis. Inside are 28 frescoes which show scenes from Saint Francis's life, painted by the famous artist, Giotto, in the 13th century.

In church

Italian Roman Catholic churches are decorated with beautiful sculptures, paintings, stained glass windows, bronze doors, and candles. During the church service, worshipers face the **altar**, from which the priest holds **mass**. Mass is the main part of the service. The priest also performs special ceremonies, such as **baptisms**, **first communions**, and **confirmations**. All these ceremonies welcome children and young adults into the Church.

A part of life

The Roman Catholic Church plays a large part in people's lives. People ask their priest for advice on personal issues. They visit shrines across the country. The shrines are devoted to Jesus, Mary, and different saints. Some people go simply to worship, but others who are sick visit in the hope that they will be cured. The Church also helps Italians by running hundreds of hospitals and charities.

At a shrine in Assisi, flowers and candles surround a statue of Jesus' mother, Mary.

People visit Italian churches to pray or to admire the beautiful paintings, statues, and stained glass windows. This is the duomo in Siena.

🏛 Vatican City 🏛

Vatican City is the headquarters of the Roman Catholic Church. Also called the Vatican and the Holy See, it is not actually part of Italy. It is its own country. At just 109 acres (44 hectares), it is one of the smallest countries in the world. The borders of Vatican City are marked by stone walls and lines painted on the streets. Inside are churches, libraries, museums, offices, gardens, and apartments — all belonging to the Roman Catholic Church. There is even a Vatican post office, radio station, and helicopter pad.

Home of the pope

Fewer than 1,000 people live in Vatican City. They include priests and other Church officials. The pope, who lives in the beautiful Vatican Palace, is the head of the tiny country. In addition to his duties as ruler of the Vatican and **bishop** of Rome, he makes important decisions about religious matters and performs holy **rituals** around the world.

Priceless treasures

Worshipers and other visitors marvel at the Vatican's beautiful, historic buildings. Many were designed by Italy's most famous **architects**. The Vatican houses one of the world's largest art collections. Thousands of pieces, from ancient Egyptian and Roman works to those of artists from the last few centuries, are found there. Some of the most famous works of art were painted on the walls and ceilings of the Sistine Chapel by the great Italian artist Michelangelo. The Vatican also has an enormous collection of ancient books, some of which date back more than 2,000 years.

(top) The enormous St. Peter's Square was built during the seventeenth century so that Christians from all over the world could gather there.

The Vatican is filled with artwork by some of the world's most famous artists, including Raphael and Michelangelo Buonarroti. This is a painting of the baby Jesus with his mother, Mary and two angels.

St. Peter's Basilica and its square

At the center of the Vatican is one of the world's largest Christian churches — St. Peter's Basilica. Completed in 1615, it took 150 years to build. The basilica is named after Saint Peter, who is believed to have been the first Roman Catholic pope. It is said that the church is built on the spot where Saint Peter was buried.

Outside the basilica is the huge round *piazza* called St. Peter's Square. Hundreds of stone pillars surround the square. On top of the pillars stand 96 large statues of saints and martyrs, Christians who were **executed** by people who wanted them to give up their religion. Hundreds of thousands of visitors crowd St. Peter's Square on special occasions to receive the blessing of the pope, who appears on a balcony above the basilica's entrance.

A massive canopy covers the altar at the center of St. Peter's Basilica.

Guarding the pope

Throughout Vatican City, troops called Swiss Guards keep watch. They are responsible for protecting the pope. Hundreds of years ago, the Vatican hired these troops from Switzerland for protection. In 1506, the Swiss troops became the pope's permanent guards.

The 100 soldiers who make up the Swiss Guards usually wear uniforms that include blue doublets, or jackets, and berets. On special occasions, they wear centuries-old uniforms of red, blue, and yellow stripes. It is said that these uniforms were designed by Michelangelo.

(right) Two Swiss Guards, wearing red, blue, and yellow uniforms, stand watch outside Vatican Palace during Easter celebrations.

(below) Thousands of people wait for the pope to perform an Easter service in St. Peter's Square.

Italians celebrate many holidays and festivals throughout the year. Some celebrations mark occasions such as the harvest season or the anniversary of an important historical event. Others are Roman Catholic holidays. For example, a Jubilee is a special celebration that the Church declares on certain years. It is a chance for Roman Catholics to visit Rome and Vatican City, and attend special ceremonies. The Jubilee in 2000 was one of the largest in history. It marked the two-thousandth anniversary of the birth of Christ.

The Christmas season

Natale, or Christmas, marks the birth of Jesus Christ. The weeks before and after *Natale* are filled with many joyful celebrations. During the nine days before *Natale*, musicians in costumes play *ciaramelle*, or bagpipes, in the streets. Special church services are also held. On the eve of *Natale*, December 24, families gather for a feast. Then, at midnight, everyone goes to a special mass that celebrates Christ's birth. The day of *Natale*, unlike the previous evening, is a quiet one for most people, who relax at home.

A musician plays **ciaramelle** *made from pigskin at a* **Natale** *celebration in Monreale, on the island of Sicily.*

Happy *Capodanno*!

A week after *Natale*, people celebrate *Capodanno*, or New Year's, with parties and fireworks. There are many *Capodanno* customs, including opening windows to let out the old year. In the south, some people even throw things, such as pots and pans, out the open windows. *Lenticcie*, or **lentils**, and *cotechino*, a type of pork sausage, are part of many *Capodanno* feasts. People believe that lentils, because of their golden color, symbolize money. Eating them will bring wealth in the new year. As for *cotechino*, it is fatty. Fat also symbolizes wealth.

To prepare for **Natale,** *people set up* **presepios** *in their homes or churches. A* **presepio** *is a Nativity scene, a set of hand-carved figures that include the baby Jesus, his parents Mary and Joseph, and the three Wise Men who visited them.*

The *Befana* gives gifts

Santa Claus, the Christmas tree, and exchanging gifts on Christmas are relatively new traditions in Italy. It is an Italian tradition instead to give gifts on January 6. This day, called the *Befana*, or Epiphany, celebrates the arrival of the three Wise Men who brought presents for the baby Jesus. On this holiday, children are told the story of an old woman named the *Befana*. When Jesus was born, she was busy working at home and was unable to visit him. Today, she flies from house to house looking for the newborn Christ. While on her search, she leaves candies and toys for good children and a lump of coal for children who misbehave. To celebrate the story of the *Befana*, children write her letters asking for gifts and people dress up like her.

Carnevale

The name *Carnevale* means "goodbye to meat." *Carnevale* is celebrated just before Lent, a 40-day period of prayer and **fasting** during which Roman Catholics often do not eat meat or rich foods. In February or March, people in towns and cities dress in fancy costumes and take part in special fairs, parades, and feasts. *Carnevale* celebrations may last anywhere from a few days to a week, depending on where they are held.

Traditions of *Carnevale*

Venice, Italy's famous city of canals, holds some of the largest *Carnevale* events. These include a long parade of **gondolas** and a grand parade to the cathedral. There are also balls, at which people wear stunning masks and clothes that look like what people wore in the 1700s.

Other *Carnevale* events include the *Sartiglia* competition. This competition has been held for hundreds of years in Oristano, on the island of Sardinia. While galloping through the street, masked horsemen try to stab their swords through a small metal star. The star is hung above the street from a wire. The more times the horsemen stab the star, the better their town's fortunes will be in the coming year.

People dress in colorful costumes and masks made from feathers, beads, and sequins during **Carnevale** *celebrations in Venice.*

Pasqua

Pasqua, or Easter, is the time when Christians remember Christ's death and his return to life. Families hold a special *Pasqua* feast of lamb, followed by special cakes and chocolate eggs. St. Peter's Square in Vatican City is the center of Italy's *Pasqua* celebrations. There, the pope holds a special church service, where he blesses hundreds of thousands of onlookers.

Florentine fireworks

People in the city of Florence celebrate *Pasqua* with the *Scoppio del Carro* or "Explosion of the Cart." A team of white oxen pulls a cart loaded with fireworks and flowers into the *piazza* in front of the city's cathedral. While the priest performs the *Pasqua* service in the cathedral, he lights a small rocket attached to a mechanical dove. The dove shoots along a wire and out the church to the cart, lighting the fireworks.

Local holidays

Each Italian city, town, and village has a holiday dedicated to a Roman Catholic saint. The saint is treated like a local hero and is said to watch over the citizens. Although the custom is fading, on their saint's holiday people sometimes dress in their good clothes or in their region's traditional costumes and go to church. Then, they hold a parade in which they carry a statue or picture of their saint through the streets. Later, a feast, games, and dances are held.

The cricket festival

People in the city of Florence celebrate the springtime with a special cricket festival, called *Festa del Grillo.* This festival takes place 40 days after *Pasqua.* Families buy crickets, whose song is a symbol of spring, at special stalls throughout town. Then, everyone gathers for games and food at Florence's Cascine Park. People believe that if their cricket is still singing by bedtime, it is a sign of good luck.

White and red smoke rises from a cart after the Scoppio del Carro *in Florence.*

A young girl chooses a brightly painted cage in the shape of a house in which she will keep her cricket for **Festa del Grillo.**

Families and friends rush to the finish line to greet riders from the **Palio**.

Siena's *Palio*

One of the most exciting local events is the *Palio*, a horserace held twice each summer — on July 2 and August 16 — in the town of Siena. The race is held in honor of Jesus' mother, Mary. The celebrations begin when riders from seventeen rival *contrade*, or areas of the city, bring their horses into the local church to be blessed by the priest. Then, they parade to the *piazza* with the townspeople, who are dressed in traditional costumes. A cart that bears the winner's prize — a silk banner which the winning *contrada* displays for a year — follows. In fact, the word *palio* means "banner."

The *Palio* takes place in the famous Piazza del Campo. The jockeys ride bareback around the *piazza* which is covered with straw, making it very slippery. Riders make hairpin turns at high speeds and are sometimes thrown from their horses! The first horse to complete three laps, with or without its rider, wins the race. The race may last only 75 seconds!

Liberation and labor

Italy's most important non-religious holiday is the *Anniversario della Liberazione*, or Liberation Day, on April 25. It celebrates the anniversary of Italy's freedom from the Germans, who occupied the country during World War II (1939–1945). *Primo Maggio*, May 1, is another significant holiday. In other countries it is called "Labor Day" or "May Day." It celebrates the hard work of Italy's millions of **laborers**. On this day, unions, or groups that protect the rights of workers, organize parades and there are often speeches and concerts.

Dressed in medieval costumes, spectators await **Primo Maggio** *celebrations in Assisi.*

Over the centuries, Italian artists have created magnificent pieces of pottery, sculpture, and painting to make their towns and cities more beautiful. Artwork is everywhere — in *piazzas*, churches, parks, and even along streets or alleys. Palaces that were once home to kings, popes, and wealthy families are now art museums.

Great art continues to be important to Italians. Experts work constantly to preserve the masterpieces of the past. Modern art is also well respected. One of the most famous international shows, the *Biennale* exhibition, is held every other year in Venice. It attracts artists and art lovers from around the world.

Ancient art

Some of Italy's oldest works of art were created by the ancient Etruscans, Greeks, and Romans who lived in the land thousands of years ago. They liked to sculpt and paint the human body and portray scenes of hunts, battles, and athletic games. They created magnificent floor mosaics, which are pictures made from small squares of colored stone and glass. They also painted frescoes, or paintings on fresh plaster, on the walls of wealthy Romans' homes and tombs.

A Roman warrior rides a horse-drawn chariot in this ancient Roman mosaic.

This mosaic, which shows Jesus Christ, is made up of hundreds of pieces of colored stone.

Christian art

Not long after Christianity began in the first century, Italians began to portray Christ, Mary, and scenes from the New Testament in their art. Their first pieces were done on the walls and ceilings of the catacombs beneath Rome. It was in these tunnels that Christians worshiped in secret. They were fleeing **persecution** from people who considered their religion dangerous.

The Renaissance

By the late 1300s, the study of ancient Roman and Greek art, architecture, and science became very popular in Italy. The next 200 years were known as the *Rinascimento* or Renaissance. Renaissance means "rebirth." The ancient Roman and Greek ideas inspired exciting new work by artists and **scholars** all over Italy and Europe. Most of the greatest Renaissance artists, including the sculptors Donatello (1386–1466) and Michelangelo (1475–1564), as well as painters Leonardo da Vinci (1452–1519) and Raffaelo, also known as Raphael (1483–1520), were Italians.

Renaissance art

Renaissance art often showed Christian subjects, but many artists also portrayed important leaders or scenes from legends. Artists based their work on the close study of the human body and the world around them. They used rich materials and vibrant colors to make their paintings more beautiful. Most of their pieces had a calm, relaxed quality to them. Renaissance artists also mastered perspective, the art of drawing objects on a flat surface to make them look three-dimensional.

(right) An angel wearing a golden halo and a richly colored dress plays the violin in this painting from the Renaissance.

(below) The **School of Athens,** *by Raphael, shows Aristotle and Plato, two important Greek philosophers, standing at the center of a room, surrounded by other philosophers from ancient Greece.*

The great Leonardo

Leonardo da Vinci is thought to be one of the most brilliant minds of all time. He was a master painter, sculptor, architect, engineer, inventor, and writer. He studied the natural world and recorded his observations in his notebooks. People still study his notebooks today. They contain detailed sketches and ideas for fantastic inventions, such as flying machines and diving suits, that were not built until centuries later. Leonardo da Vinci's paintings are known for their imagination, detail, and beauty. His *Last Supper* and *Mona Lisa* are among the most famous paintings in the world.

Like all of da Vinci's sketches and notes, his ideas for a flying machine were written backwards.

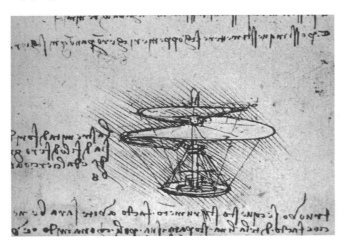

The Last Supper *shows the story from the New Testament in which Christ eats for the last time with his apostles, or followers.*

For centuries, people have been fascinated by the slight smile on the **Mona Lisa.**

The master Michelangelo

Michelangelo Buonarroti was considered the greatest artist of his day. He painted, sculpted, wrote poetry, and designed structures, including the dome of St. Peter's Basilica. Michelangelo's work is famous for its beauty, strength, and enormous size. Michelangelo's most famous paintings are the huge frescoes on the ceiling and back wall of the Sistine Chapel in Vatican City. They took eleven years to complete. The artist spent four of these years lying on his back on a scaffold, painting the ceiling!

(right) Michelangelo's **Last Judgement** *is made up of hundreds of smaller scenes, including* **Christ, the Judge, and the Virgin.** *It covers one wall of the Sistine Chapel.*

(below) **The Creation of Adam** *is on the ceiling of the Sistine Chapel.*

The Baroque style

Italian artists of the 1600s and 1700s created pieces that were full of action and excitement. Their style was called Baroque. Giovanni Lorenzo Bernini (1598–1680) was known for his sculptures in which subjects seemed to move. The master Baroque painter Caravaggio (1573–1610) created stirring drama in his works, such as the *Conversion of St. Paul*, by painting shadows side-by-side with beams of harsh light and by portraying subjects with strong emotions.

Bernini's sculpture **Apollo and Daphne** *illustrates the story of a woman who changes into a tree.*

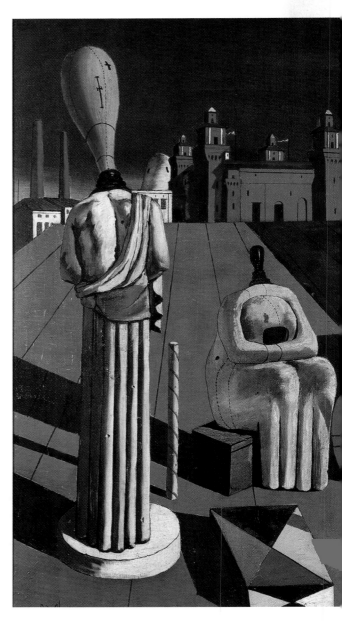

In this painting by Giorgio De Chirico, called **The Disquieting Muses**, *strange figures, shapes, and shadows fill a* **piazza**.

Modern art

In the late 1800s and early 1900s, Italian artists began to paint in a more modern style. A group of artists called the Futurists used bright colors and swirling, repeating shapes to paint machines and people in motion. Giorgio De Chirico, on the other hand, painted landscapes of a fantasy world and buildings where only shadows and **mannequins** lived. Amedeo Modigliani preferred portraits. He used bright colors to paint people with very long bodies and faces.

Architecture

Some of the greatest structures in Italy were built by the ancient Romans. Since Roman times, powerful families, rulers, and church leaders have built many other structures that were decorated with sculptures, frescoes, bronze doors, and fine marble.

The Pantheon

The Pantheon is one of Rome's best-preserved ancient buildings. Early in the second century, this temple was built in a round shape instead of the usual rectangular one. It was topped with a beautiful dome which, until 1960, was the largest dome in the world. Inside, the Pantheon is lined with colored marble and pillars. It is lit only by sunlight, which spills through the 27-foot (8-meter) wide opening in the dome's center. The Pantheon is now the burial place of famous Italians, including Italian monarchs.

(top) The Castel Sant' Angelo was once used as a fortress by popes. If the popes were attacked, defenders would pour boiling oil over the enemies through narrow slots in the castle's walls.

The height of the Pantheon's dome, from the floor to the ceiling, and the dome's diameter both measure 142 feet (43.3 meters).

Romans celebrated the Colosseum's completion with games that lasted 100 days and nights. With 80 entrances in this stadium, 50,000 spectators could get in or out in less than five minutes.

The Colosseum

Today, the enormous Colosseum sits in ruins. Once it was Rome's greatest stadium. When it was completed in 82 A.D., it seated about 50,000 spectators. They came to see the bloody duels of **gladiators** and fights between people and wild animals. On a few occasions, the center of the stadium was even flooded for battles between boats! After the Roman Empire collapsed, the Colosseum was abandoned. Its marble seats, statues, and many of its building blocks were stolen. Earthquakes and lightning further damaged the four-story building.

Great monuments

Italy's former rulers built statues, fountains, arches, columns, and other monuments to honor themselves. One of the largest monuments is the 66-foot (20-meter) Arch of Septimus Severus, in Rome. It was completed in 205 A.D. to honor the **emperor** Septimus Severus. As Romans passed under it, they were reminded of his great military victories. Rome also has two famous columns built by the emperors Trajan and Marcus Aurelius in the second century. The columns are covered with detailed scenes from the emperors' battles.

A battle rages between soldiers on one of the many sections of the Column of Trajan.

Milan's *duomo*

One of the largest and most beautiful cathedrals in all of Europe is in Milan. Construction of the Milan *duomo* began in 1386 and ended about 500 years later. On the outside are 135 tall, pointed **spires** and more than 3,000 sculptures. Visitors can view the *duomo*'s exterior from a walkway on the roof. Inside, where up to 40,000 people can worship, are 52 pillars crowned with statues of holy figures.

*(right) The people of Milan pay a special tax that goes toward the constant restorations and additions that are made to the city's **duomo**.*

(below) The Leaning Tower of Pisa has tilted about 16 feet (5 meters) to one side.

The Leaning Tower

Pisa's Leaning Tower is one of the best-known buildings in the world. It was designed to hold the bells for Pisa's cathedral. When work began on the tower in 1174, no one knew that the ground beneath one side would sink. This caused the tower to lean. By 1990, the Leaning Tower was closed to tourists because people thought it might collapse.

Since 1992, engineers have used steel, concrete, and gigantic weights to anchor the tower and keep it from leaning more. They realized, however, that the problem could be solved only by changing the ground underneath. Using a special drill to remove soil from under the tower's higher side, they have made the building tilt back into a more upright position. They have no plans, however, to make the tower stand perfectly straight. People like the way it looks!

Many of the world's most important composers, musicians, and opera singers have come from Italy. They have performed in front of large audiences who cheer wildly if they are pleased with the performance and who boo, hiss, and whistle if they are unhappy.

Writing it down

Simple songs called Gregorian chants were some of the first pieces of European music to be written down on paper. The symbols used to write the chants were invented by the Roman Catholic Church in Italy during the rule of Pope Gregory I. His rule lasted from 590 to 604. Later, Italians completed the system for writing music that is common today. Italian words are still used to describe how pieces should be played. For example, *allegro* is "fast," *andante* is "slow," and *solo* is to "play or sing alone."

Singing strings

The type of violin played by musicians today was perfected by an Italian, Antonio Stradivari (c. 1644–1737). Stradivari was a master violin, viola, and cello maker. Today, the instruments he made are still considered some of the best ever and are priceless.

At the same time that Stradivari was making instruments, composer Antonio Vivaldi was writing some of the most famous pieces of music for strings. *The Four Seasons*, his best-known work, has four parts, one for each season of the year.

The home of opera

Opera was invented in Florence in the 1500s. It is the most famous music from Italy. Each opera is like a play, but the performers sing rather than speak. The stories they tell are very dramatic, and the sets and costumes are spectacular. Italians Gioacchino Rossini (1792–1868), Giuseppe Verdi (1813–1901), and Giacomo Puccini (1858–1924) were three of the world's greatest opera composers. Verdi is especially well known for his opera *Aida*, a tragic love story of Aida, a princess of Ethiopia, and Radames, an Egyptian soldier.

Craftspeople still make violins, violas, and cellos in the tradition of Stradivari.

Luciano Pavarotti (right), a famous Italian opera singer, plays Nomorino in L'elisir d'amore, *an opera by Gaetano Donizetti.*

In this painting from the eighteenth century, a man and woman dance the **tarantella.**

Tarantula music and dance

In central and southern Italy, people play *tarantella* music on an accordion or guitar. It is accompanied by the exciting *tarantella* folk dance. Dancers spin and swirl to the music alone or with a partner. Female dancers often play a tambourine to the beat of the music, which speeds up to a frantic pace. It is said that people performed the *tarantella* centuries ago to cure tarantula bites. They believed the dance helped remove the spider's venom from their bodies.

Wireless signals

Today, all kinds of music are broadcast throughout Italy and the world with an Italian invention — the radio. It was invented by Guglielmo Marconi (1874–1937). Before Marconi's invention, people could send and receive signals only over long and bulky cables. Marconi's use of an antenna instead of cables dramatically changed the way people communicated.

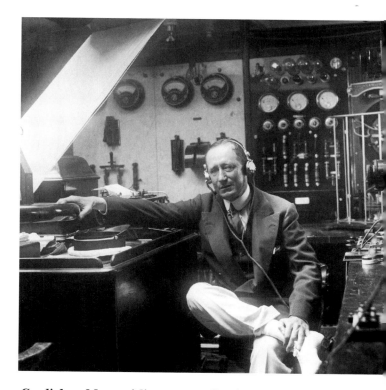

Guglielmo Marconi listens to radio signals with equipment that he invented.

Italy on stage and screen

Many Italian actors and directors have become well known around the world. Their influence on the entertainment industry has lasted for many years.

Commedia dell'arte

In the 1500s, traveling **troupes** began performing comical *commedia dell'arte* plays in Italy and throughout Europe. *Commedia dell'arte* often poked fun at people in society. The actors behaved like clowns, performing acrobatics and tricks. They wore masks with silly features such as enormous noses and huge round cheeks.

Commedia dell'arte stories are mostly improvised, or acted without scripts. They revolve around a young couple and their parents, who try to stop them from marrying. Often, the same characters appear from story to story. Old Pantalone, for example, is a father who gives endless speeches. Capitano is a cowardly soldier who loves to brag. The servant Arlecchino, called Harlequin in English, stirs up trouble with his wisecracks. Honest Pedrolino is his friend who believes everything that Arlecchino tells him.

Lights, camera, action!

Italians built a strong film industry early in the twentieth century. After World War II (1939–1945), many Italian directors and their movies began winning fans throughout the world. Some of the earliest of these films showed the difficulties of living in Italy after the war. The best known is director Vittorio De Sica's *The Bicycle Thief*. It tells the story of a struggling father and son whose only means of transportation, a bicycle, is stolen.

(top) This painting from the seventeenth century shows two **commedia dell'arte** *characters poking fun at Italian society.*

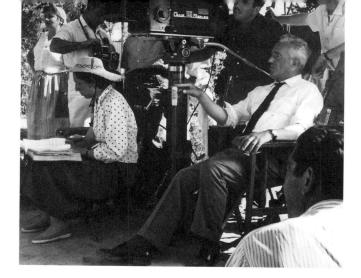

(above) *Vittorio De Sica directs actors on the set of the 1958 film* **Pan, Amory Andalucia.**

(right) *Sophia Loren signs autographs at the launch of her cookbook, in Milan.*

Fellini's vision

Later filmmakers experimented with other styles. Director Federico Fellini (1920–1993) became famous for mixing ordinary situations with dreamlike images and fantasy. Many of his films, which showed people acting in bizarre ways, told stories based on his own experiences. For example, *La Dolce Vita*, one of his best-known works, makes fun of his life in the strange world of television and movie stars.

On the big screen

Rudolf Valentino (1895–1926) was one of Italy's greatest movie stars. At the age of 18, he moved to the United States, where he played the romantic lead in several silent films of the 1920s. Valentino was adored by many fans before his sudden death at age 31.

Today, Sofia Loren is one of Italy's best-known international stars. In addition to winning an Academy Award for Best Actress in 1961 for her role in *Two Women*, she was honored with a special Academy Award in 1991 for her lifetime of achievement in Italian and American films.

(right) *Rudolf Valentino, an actor and dancer, starred in* **The Four Horsemen of the Apocalypse** *in 1921.*

Two thousand years ago, Italy's ancient Roman rulers spoke Latin. They spread this language throughout their entire empire. When the Roman Empire fell apart in the fifth century, Italy and the rest of Europe split into many different kingdoms.

The Roman Catholic Church continued to use Latin, but the rest of the people changed the language over the following centuries. With new words, expressions, and pronunciations, they created the Italian language. It is related to other languages that came from Latin — French, Spanish, Romanian, and Portuguese.

One language, many dialects

Italy was divided into many kingdoms until 1861. Each kingdom had a different dialect, or version, of Italian. It was hard for someone from Venice in the north, for example, to understand someone from Sicily in the south. When the regions of Italy united, Italians found that they needed to communicate with others from across their country. Since that time, most people have learned the Florentine dialect of Italian, which comes from Florence. They may also speak their local dialect at home or among friends.

English	Italian
Yes	*Sí*
No	*No*
Please	*Per favore*
Thank you	*Grazie*
You're welcome	*Prego*
Excuse me	*Mi scusi*
Good day	*Buon giorno*
Good evening	*Buona sera*
Good-bye	*Arrivederci*
How are you?	*Come sta?*
I don't understand	*Non capisco*
Yesterday	*Ieri*
Today	*Oggi*
Tomorrow	*Domani*
Hello/see you later	*Ciao*
Goodness!	*Mamma mia!*

A shopkeeper stands in front of racks that display Italian magazines on all subjects.

The Divine Comedy

One such work was written by Dante Alighieri (1265–1321), a poet from Florence. *The Divine Comedy* described a journey from Hell, where it is said many wicked Christians go after they die, to Paradise, the beautiful home of God. Dante's masterpiece was the first work in Italy to be written in Italian instead of Latin.

A long tradition

Since Dante's time, Italians have written important works, from essays on politics, such as *The Prince* by Niccolò Machiavelli (1469–1527), to the popular novels of modern writers Italo Calvino (1923–1985) and Umberto Eco (1932–). Several Italian writers have won Nobel Prizes in literature. Grazia Deledda (1871–1936) won in 1926. She used her native Sardinia as a setting for folktales and stories of people struggling through life. One of her most famous works, *The Woman and the Priest*, tells the heartbreaking tale of a woman whose son, a priest, falls away from the teachings of the Church.

Look at the hand gestures and facial expressions of the woman who is speaking. What do they tell about how she feels?

Body language

Many Italians use body language when they communicate. Body language is a combination of facial expressions and hand gestures. One of the most common hand gestures is to put the fingers and thumb together and hold them with the palm facing outward. This gesture asks the question "What is it?"

Italian literature

Over the centuries, Italians have written great works of literature, poetry, and **philosophy**. The roots of Italian writing go back to the ancient Romans. Latin poets, such as Virgil, Ovid, and Horace, wrote both short and long poems based on myths and legends. Later writers created literature for the Roman Catholic Church.

Dante Alighieri reads from two books written in Latin in this painting from the fifteenth century.

Italians enjoy a rich collection of folktales. They have been passed down over many generations. One of the most famous tales is *Pinocchio*, which was written in the late 1800s by Carlo Lorenzini, or Carlo Colladini as he was known. Other Italian stories, such as the one below, tell of heroes and adventurers from long ago.

The tale of precious gifts

Ansaldo of the Ormanini family was a trader from Florence. He was known for his quick thinking and generosity.

One day, while sailing the Mediterranean Sea, he stopped at an island he had never before visited. The islanders had met few Florentines, and their king and queen invited Ansaldo to a banquet.

That evening, Ansaldo was seated with the royal family in their banquet hall. "Your island and palace are beautiful," he said.

"Thank you," the queen replied, "but one thing robs us of all happiness." Ansaldo was about to ask what that was when the servants marched into the hall with mouth-watering food. As soon as they put the meal down, hundreds of rats burst in and carried it away.

"It is like this every day," the king wept. "Everything we have tried to get rid of the rats has failed!"

Ansaldo smiled. "I shall return with the solution to your problem," he said. He ran back to his ship and returned with two cats.

"What creatures are these?" asked the queen.

"They are my most valuable crew members," Ansaldo replied. "We Italians carry two on each ship. They are my gift to you." He let the cats loose and, within a few hours, they had killed all the rats. The king and queen thought they had seen a miracle.

"You saved us!" cheered the king. "In return, we will repay you with the most precious possessions on our island." Before Ansaldo set sail the next day, they brought him a chest of their finest gems.

Soon, Ansaldo returned to Florence and told this story to his friend, Giocondo de' Fifanti. Giocondo thought, "If the islanders gave Ansaldo all those gems for just two cats, imagine what treasures they would give me if I presented them with the finest gifts in all of Florence!"

So, Giocondo spent a fortune on beautiful cloth, jewelry, and artwork. He sailed to the island and gave his gifts to the king and queen. They were astounded. "You Florentines are so kind," said the queen. "We have never before seen such treasures. In return, we will repay you with the most precious possessions from our island."

The next day, as he was preparing to sail for home, Giocondo saw the king and queen leading a parade of islanders toward him. "*Mamma mia!*" he thought, "They are bringing me so many treasures that they need all their subjects to carry them!" As the procession reached Giocondo, the king said proudly, "What we give is so precious that everyone came to see you accept it."

Giocondo smiled greedily and thought, "The barrels of treasure I am about to receive will put Ansaldo to shame!" But when the gift was revealed, he gasped in shock.

There, on a pillow before him, slept two kittens that had been born to the cats left by Ansaldo.

Glossary

altar A table or stand used for religious ceremonies

architect A person who designs buildings

baptism A Christian ceremony during which a person is dipped or washed in water as a sign of washing away sin

bishop A high-ranking member of the Catholic Church

confirmation A Christian ceremony in which a person renews his or her faith and is given full membership in the Church

crucified Put to death on a cross

denomination A religious group within a faith

emperor The ruler of a country or a group of countries

execute To put to death

fast To stop eating food or certain kinds of food for religious or health reasons

first communion The Christian ceremony of receiving holy bread and wine for the first time

gladiator A slave in ancient Rome who fought at public shows

gondola A long, flat-bottomed boat used in the canals of Venice

laborer A person whose work requires strength

lentil A round seed that can be eaten

mannequin A model of a human body

mass The main ceremony of the Roman Catholic Church

persecution The act of harming another person for religious, racial, or political reasons

philosophy The study of the laws of the universe

piazza A public square in an Italian town

prophet A person who is believed to speak on behalf of a god

ritual A formal custom in which several steps are faithfully followed

saint A person through whom God has performed miracles, according to the Christian Church

scholar A very knowledgeable person

shrine A small area or structure dedicated to a god or saint

spire The pointed top of a tower

troupe A group of actors, singers, or dancers

worship To honor or respect a god

Index

1 2 3 4 5 6 7 8 9 0   Printed in the USA   0 9 8 7 6 5 4 3 2 1

Italian churches are filled with art

The Holy Roman Emperor, Frederick III, crowns Enea Piccolomine as Italy's greatest living poet.

The people are frightened when they see a miracle. What do you think has happened?

The pointed gothic arches of the cathedral in Siena.

Jesus Christ is shown carrying the cross outside the walls of Jerusalem in this church fresco.

This fresco shows the Duke of Perugia leading a procession of citizens outside his city.

Jesus Christ, angels, apostles and saints are painted high above the altar on the ceiling of a church.

Monks and nuns in Assisi

St. Francis of Assisi, who was born in 1181, was a rich man who gave away all his money to the poor and spent his life helping people. Today in Assisi, many nuns and monks follow his religious order.

A. A nun sweeps in front of her little church.

B. A nun helps a blind woman.

C. A Franciscan monk from Africa. Franciscans wear brown robes.

D. A nun walks through the old streets of Assisi.

DATE	ISSUED TO